I AM BEAUTIFUL

# I AM BEAUTIFUL

## The Words of Powerful Girls

## LATICIA NICOLE BEATTY

purposely
created
PUBLISHING

**I AM BEAUTIFUL**

Published by Purposely Created Publishing Group™

Copyright © 2020 LaTicia Nicole Beatty

Printed in the United States of America

ISBN: 978-1-64484-127-3

Special discounts are available on bulk quantity purchases by book clubs, associations and special interest groups. For details email: sales@publishyourgift.com or call (888) 949-6228.

For information logon to: www.PublishYourGift.com

I am beautiful.

I didn't always think so, and
I didn't like to look in the mirror.

Momma told me,
"Joy, you are so beautiful,"
but I did not believe her.

"No, I'm not," I said.

My skin is too dark and my braids
are too short.

None of the girls in my
class look like me.

None of the girls at my school
dress like me.

None of the girls in my ballet
class have hair like mine.

"Ashley is beautiful. She has curly brown hair and eyes the color of Grandma's hot cocoa," I said to Momma.

"What else do you like about Ashley?" Momma asked.

I told her that Ashley shares her
snacks with me.

"So she is kind?" asked Momma.

"Yes," I said.

"Do you share with Ashley?" she asked.

"Yes, of course!" I said.

"Then are you kind?"

"Yes, I guess so," I told her.

"Then you are beautiful, too,"
my mother said.

"No, I'm not,"
I told her.
"Elizabeth is beautiful.
She has golden
hair and eyes
that are blue
like the sky."

"What else do you like about Elizabeth?"
Momma asked.

I told her that Elizabeth can
count to 1,000.

"So she is smart?" Momma asked.

"Yes," I said.

"Can you count to 1,000?" she asked.

"Yes, I can!" I said.

"Then you are smart?"

"Yes, I guess so," I told her.

"So you are beautiful, too,"
my mother said.

"No, I'm not," I told her.
"Stephanie is beautiful. She has fiery
red hair and braces."

"What else do you like about Stephanie?"
Momma asked.

"Stephanie does the best tumble
in gymnastics class!"

"So she is talented?" asked Momma.

"Yes," I said.

"Can you tumble?" she asked.

"Yes, I can tumble," I told her. "But, not as good as Stephanie. I do the best splits!"

"Then you are talented?"

"Yes, I guess so," I told her.

Momma held out her hand and rubbed my cheek. "You are beautiful too, my love. I will show you."

The next day after school, Momma took me to the carnival in Pecan Park. I wanted to ride the whirl-a-round, but Momma took me to the fun house first.

We walked through a maze of rooms that had slanted floors and textured walls! The last room was a room filled with mirrors.

There were skinny mirrors, oval mirrors, curved mirrors, and even angled mirrors!

One mirror made me look short and round. Another mirror made me tall and thin. There was even a mirror on the ceiling that made my face look as wide as the room. "Aahhh," I said. "These mirrors make me look weird!"

"How do you look?" asked Momma.

"I am short and have
short ponytails."

"You are a right size with
cute, perfect ponytails."

"I guess," I said.

"What else do you see?"

"I am dark and skinny."

"You are brown and slender,"
Momma said.

"Beauty is in the eye of the beholder," Momma said. "Do you know what that means?"

I didn't know what she meant.
I shook my head.

"The other little girls are beautiful because you see things about them that you like," Momma told me.
"We each see beauty differently."

"Like the mirrors!" I said.

"When you looked in each mirror, did anything change inside of you?" she asked.

"Of course not," I said.

"You are still kind, smart, and talented, right?"

"Yes!" I said.

And guess what? There, in all the mirrors, I realized Mommy was right! My ponytails are perfect. My skin is brown and smooth.

"God made you," said Momma. "Fearfully and wonderfully. You are special to Him, inside and out. That's why He only made one of you."

"I am beautiful!" I said in the mirror.
"I am talented. I am special. I am smart!
I am Joy, fearfully and wonderfully made!"

Now, it's your turn!

What do you love about yourself?
Say it out loud.

For example:

I am smart. I am talented.


I am _____.

I am _____.

## CREATING DISTINCTIVE BOOKS
## WITH INTENTIONAL RESULTS

We're a collaborative group of creative masterminds with a mission to produce high-quality books to position you for monumental success in the marketplace.

Our professional team of writers, editors, designers, and marketing strategists work closely together to ensure that every detail of your book is a clear representation of the message in your writing.

### Want to know more?
Write to us at info@publishyourgift.com
or call (888) 949-6228

Discover great books, exclusive offers, and more at
### www.PublishYourGift.com

Connect with us on social media

@publishyourgift

CPSIA information can be obtained
at www.ICGtesting.com
Printed in the USA
LVHW071953040720
659736LV00014B/761